4/06

-2

Writing the Critical Essay

ALCOHOL

An OPPOSING VIEWPOINTS® Guide

Other books in the Writing the Critical Essay series:

Writing the Critical Essay

ALCOHOL

An OPPOSING VIEWPOINTS® Guide

William Dudley, *Book Editor*

Bruce Glassman, *Vice President*
Bonnie Szumski, *Publisher, Series Editor*
Helen Cothran, *Managing Editor*

OPPOSING
VIEWPOINTS®
SERIES

GREENHAVEN PRESS
An imprint of Thomson Gale, a part of The Thomson Corporation

THOMSON
★
™
GALE

Detroit • New York • San Francisco • San Diego • New Haven, Conn. • Waterville, Maine • London • Munich

For more information, contact
Greenhaven Press
27500 Drake Rd.
Farmington Hills, MI 48331-3535
Or you can visit our Internet site at http://www.gale.com

LIBRARY OF CONGRESS CATALOGING-IN-PUBLICATION DATA

Alcohol / William Dudley, book editor.
 p. cm. — (Writing the critical essay: an opposing viewpoints guide)
 Includes bibliographical references and index.
 ISBN 0-7377-3192-3 (lib. : alk. paper)
 1. Alcoholism. 2. Youth—Alcohol use. 3. Drunk driving. 4. Essay—Authorship.
5. Rhetoric. I. Dudley, William, 1964– . II. Series.
 HV5035 .A43 2006
 808/.066616 dc22
                                                                2005052557

CONTENTS

Section Three: Supporting Research Material

E xamining the state of writing and how it is taught in the United States was the official purpose of the National Commission on Writing in America's Schools and Colleges. The commission, made up of teachers, school administrators, business leaders, and college and university presidents, released its first report in 2003. "Despite the best efforts of many educators," commissioners argued, "writing has not received the full attention it deserves." Among the findings of the commission was that most fourth-grade students spent less than three hours a week writing, that three-quarters of high school seniors never receive a writing assignment in their history or social studies classes, and that more than 50 percent of first-year students in college have problems writing error-free papers. The commission called for a "cultural sea change" that would increase the emphasis on writing for both elementary and secondary schools. These conclusions have made some educators realize that writing must be emphasized in the curriculum. As colleges are demanding an ever-higher level of writing proficiency from incoming students, schools must respond by making students more competent writers. In response to these concerns, the SAT, an influential standardized test used for college admissions, required an essay for the first time in 2005.

Books in the Writing the Critical Essay: An Opposing Viewpoints Guide series use the patented Opposing Viewpoints format to help students learn to organize ideas and arguments and to write essays using common critical writing techniques. Each book in the series focuses on a particular type of essay writing—including expository, persuasive, descriptive, and narrative—that students learn while being taught both the five-paragraph essay as well as longer pieces of writing that have an opinionated focus. These guides include everything necessary to help students research, outline, draft, edit, and ultimately write successful essays across the curriculum, including essays for the SAT.

Using Opposing Viewpoints

This series is inspired by and builds upon Greenhaven Press's acclaimed Opposing Viewpoints series. As in the parent series, each book in the Writing the Critical Essay series focuses on a timely and controversial social issue that provides lots of opportunities for creating thought-provoking essays. The first section of each volume begins with a brief introductory essay that provides context for the opposing viewpoints that follow. These articles are chosen for their accessibility and clearly stated views. The thesis of each article is made explicit in the article's title and is accentuated by its pairing with an opposing or alternative view. These essays are both models of persuasive writing techniques and valuable research material that students can mine to write their own informed essays. Guided reading and discussion questions help lead students to key ideas and writing techniques presented in the selections.

The second section of each book begins with a preface discussing the format of the essays and examining characteristics of the featured essay type. Model five-paragraph and longer essays then demonstrate that essay type. The essays are annotated so that key writing elements and techniques are pointed out to the student. Sequential, step-by-step exercises help students construct and refine thesis statements; organize material into outlines; analyze and try out writing techniques; write transitions, introductions, and conclusions; and incorporate quotations and other researched material. Ultimately, students construct their own compositions using the designated essay type.

The third section of each volume provides additional research material and writing prompts to help the student. Additional facts about the topic of the book serve as a convenient source of supporting material for essays. Other features help students go beyond the book for their research. Like other Greenhaven Press books, each book in the Writing the Critical Essay series includes bibliographic listings of relevant periodical articles, books, Web sites, and organizations to contact.

Writing the Critical Essay: An Opposing Viewpoints Guide will help students master essay techniques that can be used in any discipline.

Background to Controversy: The Effects of Alcohol

Alcohol (also called ethyl alcohol or ethanol) is a chemical compound that is found in such beverages as beer, wine, and distilled "hard" liquor such as whiskey and gin. It is also a drug that affects the brain. Alcoholic beverages, which have been part of human civilization for thousands of years, are pervasive in today's society. An estimated two-thirds of American adults drink alcohol to some extent. More than $116 billion was spent in the United States on alcoholic beverages in 1999. Alcohol's widespread and enduring popularity, coupled with its sometimes troubling effects on a person's brain, body, and emotions, have made it a recurring public issue and a cause of public and private tragedies.

Some of the effects people experience from consuming alcohol are short-term, lasting only as long as alcohol remains in the body and immediately thereafter. Other effects are long-term and arise in people who develop an ongoing drinking habit or drug dependence. In such cases, which may take years to play out, consuming alcohol may have significant ramifications not only for people who drink but also for those around them.

Short-Term Effects of Alcohol

When a person drinks, alcohol travels to the stomach and the small intestine. From there it is absorbed into the bloodstream and carried to the rest of the body. The short-term effects of alcohol can vary depending on the person's physiology and the amount of alcohol consumed. These factors affect a person's BAC (blood alcohol concentration)—the amount of alcohol circulating in the blood. As BAC increases, so do alcohol's effects on the brain and emotions. Thus at BACs of .01 to .04 (what most adults would attain with one or two drinks), a person may feel a decrease in inhibitions and a sense of elation or relaxation. At .05 to .07 (three or four drinks), the drinker's alertness is diminished and feelings of anxiety and depression may be increased. Vision and reaction time can also be affected.

American teenagers tend to drink more frequently than they smoke cigarettes or take drugs.

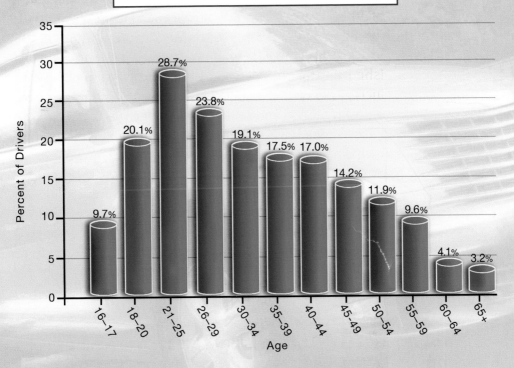

Driving Under the Influence of Alcohol, by Age

Percent of Drivers (y-axis): 0, 5, 10, 15, 20, 25, 30, 35

- 16–17: 9.7%
- 18–20: 20.1%
- 21–25: 28.7%
- 26–29: 23.8%
- 30–34: 19.1%
- 35–39: 17.5%
- 40–44: 17.0%
- 45–49: 14.2%
- 50–54: 11.9%
- 55–59: 9.6%
- 60–64: 4.1%
- 65+: 3.2%

Age (x-axis)

Source: 2003 National Survey on Drug Use and Health, Substance Abuse and Mental Health Services Administration.

At .10 (five to seven drinks), people experience clumsiness, loss of balance, and slurred speech. A person with a BAC between 0.15 and 0.20 may stumble around, insist he or she is not drunk, explode in a rage, and not remember anything later. Emotions—fear, anger, joy—may become uncontrollable. Alcohol generally causes a stupor at concentrations of 0.30 and a coma at 0.40. Death can occur at concentrations of 0.50 or more as the brain areas controlling the heart and lungs fail to function.

The body's liver metabolizes alcohol, changing it to water, carbon dioxide, and energy at about the rate of half an ounce every hour. Only time can reduce and eliminate a person's BAC after drinking. Once that is accomplished, the person is sober again, although not free from alcohol's short-term effects. Many people experience hangovers after becoming sober, with symptoms that include thirst, headache, and nausea. Some scientists attribute hangovers to low blood sugar; others to fluid retention in the brain.

In addition to affecting one's physical and emotional state, alcohol intoxication can influence a person's behavior and actions. In many instances alcohol simply creates a positive mood and sense of well-being. However, in some cases losing one's inhibitions can result in behaviors and incidents that may cause later embarrassment—or worse. Some people become silly, sad, or depressed while intoxicated, while others may become angry, argumentative, aggressive, or even violent. Alcohol may lead to unplanned sexual encounters, facilitate date rape, or cause people to engage in fights or criminal activities. A 1987 study of youths held in juvenile detention halls revealed that near-

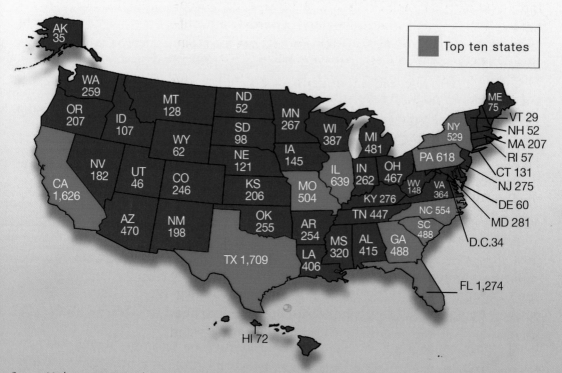

Alcohol-Related Traffic Fatalities by State*

Top ten states

AK 35
WA 259
OR 207
ID 107
MT 128
ND 52
MN 267
WI 387
MI 481
ME 75
VT 29
NH 52
MA 207
RI 57
NY 529
PA 618
CT 131
NJ 275
NV 182
UT 46
CO 246
WY 62
SD 98
NE 121
IA 145
IL 639
IN 262
OH 467
WV 148
VA 364
DE 60
MD 281
CA 1,626
KS 206
MO 504
KY 276
NC 554
AZ 470
NM 198
OK 255
AR 254
TN 447
SC 488
D.C. 34
MS 320
AL 415
GA 488
TX 1,709
LA 406
FL 1,274
HI 72

Source: Mothers Against Drunk Driving/National Traffic Safety Administration, 2003. *Numbers last updated for 2003.

ly a third of them were under the influence of alcohol when they were arrested. In worst-case scenarios, alcohol may result in behavior that leads to people getting killed. Experts have estimated that alcohol use is responsible for one hundred thousand deaths each year in the United States. Many of these deaths are motor vehicle fatalities, but alcohol abuse also contributes to injuries and deaths from falls, drowning, fires, and violence.

Alcoholism and Other Long-Term Effects

In addition to these short-term influences, alcohol can have several long-term effects on one's physical health, mental state, and relationships with other people. Heavy drinking can impinge upon one's health in several ways. These include cirrhosis and other disorders of the liver, which are believed responsible for thousands of deaths each year. Continued heavy drinking is also linked with damage to the stomach, intestines, and pancreas, as well as various brain disorders and cancers of the mouth and esophagus. Pregnant women who drink alcohol also run the risk of harming their children. Babies exposed to alcohol in utero may develop fetal alcohol syndrome and suffer from mental retardation and abnormalities of the brain, face, and feet.

Some people become dependent on alcohol to the extent that their physical and mental health is imperiled, as well as their relationships with other people. The National Institute on Alcohol Abuse and Alcoholism has estimated that almost 14 million people have alcohol problems, and that 8.1 million of these people suffer from alcoholism. In the nineteenth and early twentieth centuries, people who abused alcohol were believed to be weak and lack moral character. That view has evolved over the past century. Alcoholism is now considered by most as a disease—a condition characterized by the repeated and uncontrollable use of alcohol despite negative consequences. Other symptoms include nausea, shakiness, anxiety when a person stops drinking, and the buildup of tolerance for alcohol, increasing the amount of alcohol necessary to get drunk. Recent research has pursued the possibility that alcoholism—which often runs in families—may have a genetic component. The idea that alcoholism is a disease has transformed how the medical establishment and society in general has treated alcoholics.

Many alcoholics tell similar stories of addiction. They initially try alcohol for a variety of reasons—to satisfy their curiosity, alleviate mental anxiety, or boost their self-esteem. Finding that alcohol makes them feel better leads them to drink regularly. Sometimes they are able to maintain their previous routines; other times they drop out of school or lose a job or a spouse and continue to drink. They go through a stage of denial in which they insist they do not have a drinking problem even as constant drinking is wrecking their lives. Their denial is finally overcome, either through "hitting bottom" through some alcohol-related calamity or through the "intervention" of family members and others, who confront them about their alcohol problem. They then enter treatment and counseling programs where they work to stop their drinking. Alcoholism, most believe, can be treated but not cured; one is always a "recovering alcoholic."

Alcohol and Public Policy

The social and health problems created by the misuse of alcohol have long been a focus of public controversy. The United States went so far as to amend the Constitution in 1919 to prohibit the sale and manufacture of alcoholic beverages. That social experiment did not have the intended effect of stopping alcohol consumption and its related problems. Many people defied the law, leading to a flourishing organized crime scene. Few if any people call for a return to Prohibition, which was repealed in 1933, but debates continue on how and how much to regulate certain aspects of alcohol consumption. One major point of contention is the drinking age. In the 1970s many states

A federal agent destroys barrels of confiscated rum during the Prohibition era.

lowered the age to eighteen. However, by 1988 all states had raised the drinking age to twenty-one to combat youth alcohol problems and alcohol-related traffic fatalities. The viewpoints in the following section provide a sampling of opinions and stories about people's experiences with alcohol and the positive and negative consequences of alcohol use and abuse.

Section One: Opposing Viewpoints on Alcohol

Youth Drinking Is a Serious Problem

Stephen Fraser

Stephen Fraser writes for *Current Health 2*, a monthly publication about health and fitness issues. In the following viewpoint he tells the story of Karen, a person who started drinking heavily at age fourteen and battled alcohol addiction for several years. Karen was eventually able to turn her life around with the help of Alcoholics Anonymous (AA). Fraser uses Karen's story as an example of the problem of youth drinking—a problem that he says affects millions of people.

Consider the following questions:

1. What reasons did Karen give for drinking, according to Fraser?
2. How many teens in the United States are regular drinkers, according to the author?
3. What different treatment programs and methods did Karen try?

Karen, 17, had her first drink at age 4. The occasion was Passover, a Jewish holiday marked by the ceremonial drinking of a glass of sweet wine. But the drink was too much for Karen to handle. "I got drunk and fell down and twisted my ankle!" she said.

During the next 10 years, Karen, who lives in New York City, continued to drink on and off in secret. At age 14, she started drinking heavily—pretty much every day for nine months straight. To hide her drinking, she lied to family

Teenage alcohol abuse can cause relationships to deteriorate, creating rifts between parents and children.

and friends. Her relationship with her parents, which had always been close, quickly deteriorated. Doors were always slamming. Her father became extremely angry. When her parents set a curfew, she came in hours later.

Some people have a "bright-light experience when they drink," Karen told *Current Health*. They feel better, happier—"Everything lifts," she said. Karen never felt that way. Drinking wasn't something that helped her escape her troubles. (She was struggling with clinical depression.) Drinking was something she couldn't control. Her body had become physically dependent on alcohol.

A study by the National Institute on Alcohol Abuse and Alcoholism (NIAAA) found that people who begin drinking at age 15 or younger are four times more likely to become addicted to alcohol than people who begin drinking in adulthood.

Karen's experience isn't unique. According to NIAAA, between 3 million and 7 million teens ages 14 to 17 are regular drinkers and have a confirmed alcohol problem.

One out of five eighth-grade students has probably had a drink in the past 30 days. Those are sobering numbers.

Coming Clean

After nine chaotic months, Karen was finally confronted by her parents. She came clean about her addiction and felt enormous relief at having told them. She entered an outpatient program, where she met other teenagers who had alcohol or drug addictions.

Although attending the outpatient program was helpful, Karen said she still felt lost and suicidal. So her parents checked her into a psychiatric hospital, where she attended her first Alcoholics Anonymous (AA) meeting. She relapsed three times over the next few months. One morning, after finishing off a bottle of whiskey the night before, she woke up lying in her own vomit.

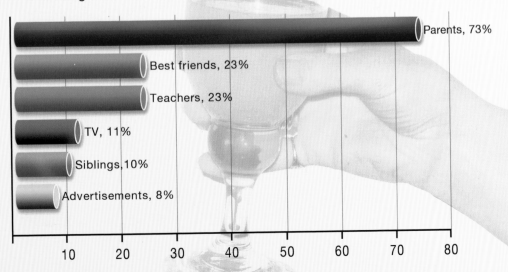

What Influences American Youth's Decisions About Drinking?

- 73 percent of American youth (ages 8–17) identified their parents as a leading influence on their decisions about drinking. *

Parents, 73%
Best friends, 23%
Teachers, 23%
TV, 11%
Siblings, 10%
Advertisements, 8%

10   20   30   40   50   60   70   80

Source: Roper Youth Report, 2003. *More than one response accepted.

During the next two years, however, Karen's life began to turn around. In AA, she met teens as well as adults with drinking problems. When she first started attending AA, Karen thought her life was over. But gradually, she began to take control of her addiction.

Moving Forward

One of the principles of AA is that helping other alcoholics is essential for getting—and staying—sober. That is what Karen is doing today. "I am at the point at AA meetings where I go to support others," she said. [In the summer of 2004] she broadened her outreach beyond alcoholics and worked at a nonprofit organization for women.

Karen doesn't touch alcohol anymore, and her relationship with her parents is 100 percent better. "I have a very loving, trusting relationship with my parents now, for the first time in years," she said.

Gamble. © 1986 by King Features Syndicate. Reproduced by permission.

What advice does Karen have for teens who have drinking problems? She tells them to consider a rehabilitation program or AA. Many of her friends have been helped by rehab, and AA meetings for young people take place all over the United States. "Check it out," she said. "You don't have to do anything you don't want to. There are suggestions but not strict rules."

Karen is a high school senior this year [2004] and is thinking ahead to college. Her voice carries a note of optimism. She knows that life holds many opportunities. "And I'm actually having fun!" she added.

Alcoholics Anonymous and other rehabilitation programs allow teen alcoholics to share their experiences.

Analyze the essay:

1. Who does the author want to read this article?
2. How does focusing on just one person help the author make his point?

The Problem of Youth Drinking Has Been Exaggerated

Laura Vanderkam

In 2002 the Harvard School of Public Health released the results of a survey of college students, finding that 44 percent of them had admitted to "binge drinking" within the previous two weeks. The authors of the study argued that these findings are evidence of a serious public health problem. In the following viewpoint Laura Vanderkam disputes this conclusion, drawing in part from her own stories and experiences of drinking while attending college. She argues that drinking did not cause problems for her or her friends, and that most college students drink responsibly. Following her graduation from Princeton University, Vanderkam worked as an intern for *USA Today*.

Consider the following questions:

1. What long-term effects did drinking have on Vanderkam and her friends?
2. What problems does the author have with the definition of "binge" drinking?
3. According to Vanderkam, how many students have required medical attention because of drinking?

By day, the historic eating clubs on Princeton's Prospect Avenue are staid mansions, but come Saturday night, kegs flow in their bustling taprooms until early in the morning. In college, drawn by bands and DJs, my friends

Harvard University students enjoy an evening of drinks and conversation at a popular local bar.

and I flocked to these campus beacons. We'd sip a "pre-party" cocktail while getting ready to go out, then drink three or so beers during the course of the night. We'd travel from club to club dancing, then amble home a few hours before dawn.

According to Henry Wechsler of the Harvard School of Public Health, we all had a drinking problem.

"The drinking style on campus is still one of excess," he said in releasing a [2002] study that found that 44% of students "binge drink"—defined by researchers as four drinks a night for women and five for men, once in the past two weeks. "We consider this to be a serious public-health problem," he said, perhaps necessitating bans on pitcher specials and happy hours. The American Medical Association [AMA] entered the fray, too, urging action against tour operators who sell booze-fests to college kids on spring break in Mexico.

What Happened to Us?

But before we ban fun, this "drinking problem" needs a closer look. My friends and I didn't get in trouble with the law. We didn't drink and drive. Our binge drinking was such a crisis that we had to settle for A averages and good jobs after graduation.

In other words, not much of a problem at all. The worst that happened to most of us because of drinking was a hangover.

But that doesn't matter to the army of busybodies intent on finding fault with student alcohol consumption. Certainly some students, like some adults, have problems with substance abuse. But the scope of the problem is much more limited than the alarmists lead people to believe.

Teach Responsible Drinking

Like most things in life, alcohol can be abused. But abuse is best discouraged by teaching people to drink responsibly.

Doug Bandow, "Alcohol Abuse Study Is Junk Science," *Conservative Chronicle*, March 20, 2002.

Defining Binge Drinking

First, what exactly is binge drinking? Every student knows the mantra "four drinks for women, five for men," but more tricky are the reasons for this standard. Why not five or six? An earlier report noted that "if the five-drink definition were used, only 3% of women college students would be classified as binge drinkers." This was a yawn of a finding, so the limit was bumped to four, for a newsworthy 41% rate. This supposedly reflects the prevalence of "alcohol-related problems." Sample problems: Arguing with friends or doing something you regret. I've done both sober.

Then there's semantics. When people hear "binge," they think "drunk." But with a tolerance, four drinks over a long night will barely induce a buzz. As long as the drinker doesn't drive impaired, it's a completely arbitrary standard chosen more for headlines than meaning. With the four/five-drink standard, a full 35% of those who choose substance-free dorms still fall in the binge category, suggesting a formula flaw.

As for the "serious public-health problem," aren't the alarmists a bit late to the party? I don't know when Harvard's Wechsler or the AMA board went to school, but chances are the drinking style was "one of excess" then, too. While baby-boomer parents may be alarmed by their children's exploits, surely they remember what college was like — or don't, which makes the point more. And boomers didn't invent excess. Gin-steeped F. Scott Fitzgerald novels suggest that Princeton students drank long before anyone studied the phenomenon.

And why not? "Youth comes but once in a lifetime," Longfellow said, and soon enough, today's college students will be bound to the earth by mortgages and rug rats. A few years of craziness, binge drinking included,

College students drink beer at a fraternity-house party.

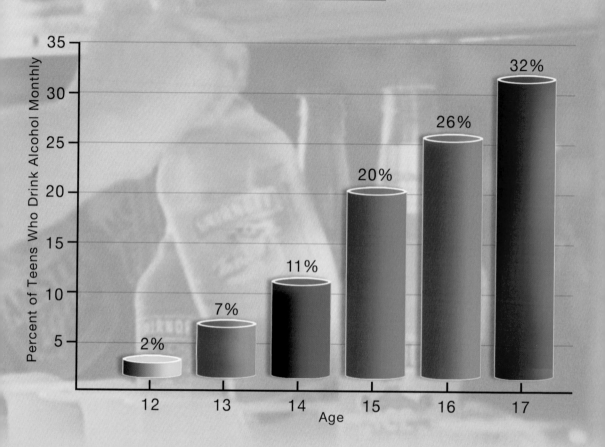

Teen Alcohol Use

Percent of Teens Who Drink Alcohol Monthly

- 12: 2%
- 13: 7%
- 14: 11%
- 15: 20%
- 16: 26%
- 17: 32%

Age

Source: National Household Survey on Drug Abuse, 2000.

are the fleeting privilege of youth. Everyone needs stories, and college is perfect for creating them by streaking or dancing on bars. If you're blessed with common sense, you can emerge unscathed.

Alarmism About Alcohol

Still, the alarmists persist. Certainly alcohol can be abused, and some students do have troubles. More accurate than the widely touted 44%, however, are statistics on drinkers' actions. Fewer than 1% have required medical attention. Fewer than 7% have been in trouble with campus or public police, and this would be lower still without an idiotically high drinking age (usually 21) that makes criminals of harmless imbibers.

Then, too, the alarmism is typical of a uniquely American hang-up. With our vices, we can do nothing halfway. We pontificate against or prohibit our secret, widespread indulgences—including alcohol.

Yet most students who drink do so responsibly, and surely four drinks, once a week, still meets that definition. It's a testament to student sensibility, despite the law. In fact, only 4% of students say they are even heavy drinkers. Denial? Perhaps, but more likely it's the alarmists, and not the Saturday night revelers, who are in denial about a "problem" that's under control.

Analyze the essay:

1. Do you believe Vanderkam's experiences, as related in the first paragraph, constitute responsible drinking? Why or why not?

2. In using Henry Longfellow's line "youth comes but once in a lifetime," what point is Vanderkam trying to make?

3. The viewpoint and stories are focused on college-aged youth. Do you believe her experiences and arguments are relevant to high school and younger youth? Why or why not?

Alcoholics Anonymous (AA) Can Help Alcoholics

Mark Warnat

Alcoholics Anonymous (AA) is a popular self-help organization whose members meet regularly in small groups to support each other in their battle against alcoholism. Participants follow a twelve-step program in which they admit to being powerless over alcohol and turn their lives over to a "higher power." In the following viewpoint, Mark Warnat, a physician's assistant, describes what happened to him when he attended an AA meeting as an observer. He describes the setting and the people, what they say and do, and his own insights into how and why AA works for people struggling with substance abuse. Warnat addresses his article to other physician's assistants, concluding that they and other health care providers should view AA as a valuable resource for helping patients battling alcohol addiction.

Consider the following questions:

1. What was the first thing that stood out for Warnat regarding the AA meeting?
2. What are the realizations that Warnat comes to over the course of the meeting?
3. What did the author find especially noteworthy about Paul's speech?

The AA meeting was held in a stuffy basement filled with circa-1970s multicolored plastic chairs lined up in neat little rows in the middle of the floor. The fluorescent lighting and the color of the walls bathed everything

Mark Warnat, "One Day at a Time," *Journal of the American Academy of Physician Assistants*, vol. 18, January 2005. Copyright © 2005 by Advanstar Communications, Inc. All rights reserved. Reproduced by permission.

in a yellow hue; everyone, including me, had a somewhat jaundiced appearance. It was a nonsmoking meeting, but the pungent aroma permeating the room made it obvious that many chain-smoking alcoholics have attended meetings in this basement. The function of the two tiny windows flanking the basement was suspect since they were not designed to open and they also did not provide much light. A coffeepot endlessly percolated in the background, and almost everyone in the basement was clutching a steaming foam cup.

The first thing that stood out is that no fewer than 40 people were attending this meeting—a meeting happening in the middle of the day, on a random Tuesday, in a midsize

It is estimated that one in every thirteen Americans has an alcohol problem.

suburb of Boston. They appeared to represent a cross section of society. They were men and women, black and white, tall and short, fat and thin, young and old. Some wore suits, crisp white shirts, paisley ties, and silk vests. Some had dirt under their fingernails and torn jeans. Some looked like the stereotypical alcoholic—strung out, unkempt, constantly fidgeting, tapping their feet, shifting in their chairs. But others looked as calm and cool as the other side of the pillow, with everything seemingly under control.

At this point I came to my own sobering realization— the first of several I would have that day—that we all have the potential to become better healers if we can eliminate our own preconceived notions and prejudices about patients based on their outward appearance.

Paul's Story

This particular meeting, according to the booklet I received in the mail from Alcoholics Anonymous, was designated as an open speaker session. In the front of the room, behind a rickety metal desk, sat a middle aged man wearing an Aeropostale sweatshirt and a baseball cap. His midsection was a bit pudgy, a striking contrast to the gaunt face.

Peering out from behind the curled brim of his cap, he began the meeting in the customary way: "Hi," he said. "I'm Paul, and I'm an alcoholic." The reply—"Hi, Paul!"— was quick and amplified from his one voice to our 40.

Paul started off by saying that he was nervous since this was the first time he had ever led a meeting. Paul's voice quivered, either from nerves or as a side effect of choking back the sadness that alcoholism had thrust upon his life. Probably it was from a bit of both. He told us how in 1999, after one of his usual drinking binges, he blacked out and lost an entire day. He described how from that day on, he battled the disease of alcoholism by attending up to six AA meetings a day. He mentioned how much he needed these meetings because alcohol and drug abuse had alienated him from his family. He spoke of how much he missed his wife and children and how he hoped

that, over time, they would be reintegrated into his newly established world of sobriety.

Throughout his gut-wrenching speech, Paul took full responsibility for his circumstances. He didn't blame anyone—not his wife, his children, his former boss, Sam Adams, Jose Cuervo, Captain Morgan, Osama Bin Laden, God, or the economy. He was contrite. He blamed himself, and he was trying his best to make amends for the wrongs he had done and to slay his personal demons.

Many alcoholics depend on Alcoholics Anonymous meetings and counseling sessions to help them avoid drinking relapses.

Celebrating Sobriety

Paul talked for about 15 minutes before opening the floor to other attendees. Seven people used the remainder of the hour to tell their own stories. Each had an equally awful tale of how the bottle, the needle, or the pill case led to their downfall. Some finished their monologue on a happy note, speaking of redemption and blissful reunions. Others did not.

'All bottles seem to be labelled "Drink Me".'

After the open forum came an announcement that the group would now give brightly colored poker chips to those who had been able to go a certain period of time without abusing. These chips were small trinkets to mark a milestone in sobriety. The chip itself was worth a fraction of a penny, yet what it represented was invaluable. "Nine months . . . nine months . . ." was yelled out. Two women walked to the front of the room and, sheepishly yet proudly, grabbed the little plastic representation of their hard work. Everyone in the room cheered exuberantly. "Six months?" came next. "Six months? . . . Three months? . . . Two months? . . . Two months? . . ." Yet nobody stood to receive a chip. After a moment, the speaker continued: "Finally, and perhaps most important of all, 24 hours without a drink?" One woman stood, grabbed the token without making eye contact with anyone in the room, and quickly sat back in her seat, squirreling away her prized possession. She got the most rousing round of applause of all.

When the room finally settled down, the speaker asked one final question. "To prove that AA and these meetings work, can we get a show of hands from those who have been clean and sober for a year or more?" Over half of the attendees raised a hand, and more sounds of applause spread through the room.

A Resource for Physician's Assistants (PAs)

At this point I had my second sobering realization. Alcoholics Anonymous does indeed work for people with addictions to alcohol and other substances of abuse, and the phone number for the nearest AA support group is a tool that PAs should consider as important as our ophthalmoscope or stethoscope. Local AA contact numbers should be a part of the vigilant clinician's repertoire, as it is our duty to find every possible resource and offer it to those in need.

As I think back on this experience, what really stands out is how accepting the people at this meeting were of each other. It is almost tragically beautiful that without hesitation, young embraced old, black embraced white, straight embraced gay, and all the categories and differences that segregate people in the "real world" melted away in that dirty, smelly basement. These strangers who shared this disease called alcoholism, who shared this awful experience, who shared this addiction and the pain that always accompanies it, seemed no longer to see race, creed, or color when looking at their fellow addicts. The outer shell that usually defines a person was stripped away, leaving a simple common core of someone battling to stay sober, one day at a time. These people were not looking for miracles. They were not looking to take giant leaps. They were simply looking to live life on life's terms while resisting the urge to escape into the bottom of a bottle.

Analyze the essay:

1. Warnat begins the article with a detailed description of the setting. What do you believe is the intended effect of his introductory paragraphs?
2. What conclusions does Warnat come to at the end of the article? Do you believe they are supported by what he has described in his essay? Why or why not?

Alcoholics Anonymous (AA) Does Not Help Alcoholics

Lilian MacDonald and Murdoch MacDonald

Lilian MacDonald and Murdoch MacDonald are a married couple residing in Scotland. They have battled drinking problems for much of their lives. In the following viewpoint, taken from a press release by the couple while promoting their Web site and book manuscript, they tell their own story of how they repeatedly tried Alcoholics Anonymous (AA) meetings but came to the conclusion that AA's ideas were inadequate and outdated. After hitting bottom and finding themselves temporarily homeless, they were finally able to cure their alcoholism by addressing problems experienced in childhood. They criticize AA's insistence on abstinence for recovering alcoholics, arguing that they have progressed enough to be able to drink socially.

Consider the following questions:

1. What problems do the MacDonalds have with AA?
2. What happened to the authors after hitting "rock bottom" ten years ago?
3. Why is media coverage generally favorable to AA, according to the MacDonalds?

Many alcoholics CAN recover and drink safely again, if and when they so wish.

Lilian and Murdoch MacDonald, "Alcoholics Can Recover and Learn to Drink Safely Again," press release, June 1, 2004. Reproduced by permission.

A Message of Hope

That is the message of hope offered on two Internet websites hosted by a Scots couple whose lives were devastated by alcoholism, but have now recovered so completely that they now not only lead normal lives again, but are also able to drink in a perfectly sociable manner once more.

That diametrically contradicts the teaching of Alcoholics Anonymous, and of many alcoholism treatment centres throughout the world. But Lilian and Murdoch MacDonald of Ayr in Scotland believe that the 12-step programme of lifelong sobriety is not the solution to alcoholism, as it only treats the symptoms and not the causes of the problem, and is merely a damage-limitation exercise.

Lilian and Murdoch argue that alcoholism, like other self-harming disorders including bulimia, anorexia and self-mutilation, is a behaviour problem, not a disease, often stemming from problems experienced in childhood. And if these problems can be identified and properly addressed, then the problem behaviour can be cured.

Rock Bottom

Ten years ago the couple had hit rock bottom, sleeping rough for two weeks on the streets of Cambridge, where a quarter of a century previously as an undergraduate Murdoch had received an honours degree in English Literature. They had moved there from Ayr with the idea of Murdoch doing research for a doctorate (PhD), but reverted to their old habits, started binge drinking, and were thrown out of their lodgings.

After a fortnight, and when they were just about at the end of their tether, two nurses on their way home after a Saturday night out took pity on Lilian and Murdoch, bought them a cup of tea and found them a place in a homeless hostel.

The couple spent the next twelve months there getting to the roots of their alcoholism. They tried AA one last time, before concluding that it was a quasi-religious

cult whose ideas on alcoholism were inadequate and out-dated.

Instead, by reading psychology, they decided that the causes of their alcoholic behaviour lay in problems experienced during childhood. And that once these problems were realised and addressed, there was no longer any need for escape through alcoholism, and they could even drink normally like other people again.

Ten years after selling newspapers from a stand in Market Square, Cambridge, so that he and Lilian could get back on their feet financially, Murdoch now writes his own regular column in the local weekly paper and also runs his own public relations consultancy.

And Lilian is so keen to pass on the benefits of their experience to others who still have problems with alcohol, that the couple are building a website www.alcoholics candrinksafelyagain.com to spread their message of hope. . . .

Earlier Critics

The couple recognise that they are not the first to criticise AA and advocate that alcoholics can make a complete recovery without having to commit themselves to a lifetime of abstinence. Indeed as long ago as 1964, Dr Arthur H Cain published an article in the *Saturday Evening Post* in which he claimed that even then "Alcoholics Anonymous had become a dogmatic cult that blocks medical progress and hampers many members' lives," and that "because of its narrow outlook, Alcoholics Anonymous prevents thousands from ever being cured. Moreover AA has retarded

'It's your drinking Derek . . . it's beginning to affect me.'

Reproduced by permission of *The Spectator*.

scientific research into one of America's most serious health problems." And more recently, Dr Stanton Peele has criticised the AA movement in his books and on his website www.peele.net. . . .

Whether people with alcohol abuse problems can ever resume social drinking is a matter of debate.

Lilian and Murdoch find it strange that since Arthur Cain's groundbreaking article in 1964, the media have appeared reluctant to give any significant coverage to people who are critical of AA. As Murdoch points out: "The media have traditionally granted AA a quasi-monopoly in the field of alcoholism, and those of us who want to promote a more enlightened and progressive

attitude towards the subject find it almost impossible to be heard. It is as if too many AA members and sympathisers have attained positions of influence in the media, and are able to censor any opinions that appear to contradict the AA philosophy." . . .

Lilian concludes: "When our ideas about alcoholism—of which we are the living proofs—gain more acceptance worldwide, and if more government money is put into preventative measures, not only will alcoholics stand a greater chance of getting back to normality, but we will also have taken the first step towards ensuring that alcoholism can be stamped out altogether."

Analyze the essay:

1. Lilian and Murdoch MacDonald wrote this viewpoint to promote their Web site and their book. Does this information affect the way you interpret their essay?
2. What details do the authors provide on how they were able to overcome their alcohol addiction problems? Do they do enough, in your view? Why or why not?

Antabuse Medication Can Help Alcoholics

Anonymous

Antabuse (disulfiram) is a drug that causes severe nausea and vomiting in people who consume alcohol. Some alcoholics take it to prevent the urge to have another drink. In the following viewpoint, a woman tells of her experiences over a period of fifteen years battling alcoholism. With the help of Antabuse, she was able to break her drinking habit.

Consider the following questions:

1. What family background did the author come from?
2. What were some of the reasons the author resorted to drinking?
3. Why was Antabuse able to help her alcoholism habit, according to the author?

I am the child of two alcoholics. I grew up with drinking alcohol as a common, accepted behavior. I enjoyed drinking in college and as a young working adult. Then I married an alcoholic. He was able to drink heavily at night and go to work every morning. While I did not drink as heavily as he did, I drank with him in the evenings for lack of anything better to do.

On My Own

After more than 20 years of this my husband became violent, and I was forced to leave. It was a profound relief when I found a suitable apartment, but now I had many

Anonymous, "How Antabuse Eased My Road to Recovery," *Addiction Professional*, vol. 2, September 2004. Copyright © 2004 by Manisses Communications Group. Reproduced by permission.

new responsibilities. First, I had to find a job. While I have a wonderful education, the jobs for which I was educated were not open to me because I had been out of the job market for so long.

I had no choice but to accept a low-level, unchallenging job that left me feeling humiliated by the end of the day. So I continued to drink. Every day after work I drove straight to the liquor store. I didn't drink massive quantities like many people do, but I would drink to get blasted. I drank alone. I didn't drink in bars. My drinking was very much a solitary, private activity. I drank socially, but then I'd go home and drink seriously.

People taking Antabuse experience severe nausea and vomiting when they drink alcohol.

As time passed, I began to wake up anxious and afraid. I was going through a tough divorce, I was very angry with my husband, my job was miserable, and I was worried about my finances and my future in general. I had been in talk therapy for a while; now I spent each session weeping. In addition to all these external events, I knew that a lot of my distress had to do with my emotional makeup, my belief system about how people interact with each other, what my expectations should be of the world, and where I fit in.

I have fought my weight all my life, and decided that maybe a nutritionist could help me. During my initial visit, I told her I was very depressed, crying all the time and waking up afraid. I also told her that I was drinking

Antabuse is one of several medications that doctors can prescribe for people battling alcoholism.

a lot, although I wanted to cut down. I then asked her if she could help me with food choices that would be in support of my trying not to drink. Instead of telling me to eat more vitamin B, which is what I expected, she was smart enough to say, "Forget about the nutrition. Talk to your doctor about your drinking and depression and call me after you have done so."

Getting in a Program

The next day, a Friday, I saw my internist and she said, "Let's get you in a program." Immediately, she phoned the hospital and arranged for me to get into a program the following Monday.

I arrived at 8 o'clock, ready for the program, but instead had to face hours of hassle with my insurance. It was just horrific. I decided, during that long frightening morning, that if my insurance wouldn't cover the program I would drive to the liquor store and just go home and give up. Finally, around 1:30 in the afternoon, I met with a doctor, and he told me the insurance would support the program. After we had talked a little he said, "You seem to me to be a perfect candidate for Antabuse."

I was astounded! I know it sounds comical now, but at that time I felt like, "Oh! I'm good for something! I'm a perfect candidate for something!" As I listened, enormously hopeful, he explained Antabuse and its actions and reactions to me and I said, "I'll take that in a heartbeat. Of course I'll take it."

Antabuse

The first time I took Antabuse, I felt relief wash over me. I suddenly felt a sense of shared responsibility, as if some other agent or some other entity was shouldering part of

Antabuse is a drug that works by interfering with the way the body metabolizes alcohol.

this problem. There was inevitability about it, a sense that this problem was really out of my hands now. I've swallowed it, and now there is nothing I can do about it.

For the first three months, I did think I would take it forever. I couldn't imagine that I could resist drinking without it, because I had tried to stop so many times over the past 15 years or so, and I never made it more than three or four weeks. But by about seven or eight months along, I noticed that I sometimes forgot to take it.

For me, the deterrent was not the fear of getting sick if I drank. It was more that I drank to seek comfort, to escape misery, and if drinking with Antabuse was going to make me sick, then I was not going to get the relief I was seeking. If I'm going to be throwing up or experiencing palpitations, I'm just going to be in a different kind of pain. So taking Antabuse meant that I simply had to sit it out, or find comfort somewhere other than the liquor store.

This program was exactly the right thing for me. There is a great instructional program with seminars on everything you need to know from assertiveness training to the 12-steps. I was supported by the instructors, by the other people who were trying to get sober, and by seeing my doctor every day. And every day I would take the Antabuse. It takes months to form new habits and to have the ability to say I can't choose to drink. So, the beauty of Antabuse is that it makes the decision for you until you can develop new coping skills for yourself. With Antabuse, I didn't feel I was fighting alone anymore.

While I no longer take Antabuse every day, I keep a bottle of it on hand just so that I know it's there if I need it. Even though I'm not taking the Antabuse at the moment, alcohol is no longer an option. Antabuse gave me the time I needed to form new ways of thinking, and now I know that alcohol is no longer an option for me.

Analyze the essay:

1. Does telling her story in the first person make the author's story more believable or compelling, in your opinion? Why or why not?
2. What details in the story does the author include that strengthen her argument that Antabuse has been helpful for her?

Alcoholics and Problem Drinkers Should Have a Variety of Treatment Options

Susan Brink

Susan Brink is a reporter for *U.S. News & World Report*. The following viewpoint interweaves the story of a person battling alcoholism with passages calling for flexible treatment options for alcoholics. The person profiled had insurance that paid for a ninety-day treatment program. Other alcoholics, Brink writes, might respond better to residential treatment programs, medications, or Alcoholics Anonymous (AA) meetings. To save money, Brink concludes, employers should provide a variety of treatment options for their employees.

Consider the following questions:

1. How much does alcoholism cost American businesses, according to Brink?
2. What is the link between geography and alcoholism treatment, according to the author?
3. Why does Brink call Lynn Cooper lucky?

Lynn Cooper knew it as she stood in the glow of the refrigerator light against the early evening darkness. She knew it as the warmth of her house penetrated her winter coat and hat, knew it as she reached for the wine bottle in her still-gloved, trembling hand. She knew—as she greedily poured the first of the evening's multiple glasses of wine—that she had a serious drinking problem. "I was standing there with a full glass of wine in my hand," she recalls, "and I hadn't even taken my gloves off."

When she had her epiphany 14 years ago, she was a company vice president. She supervised a large staff. She made a lot of money. As she says: "I was a functional alcoholic."

But often, particularly on Mondays, she didn't function well at all. She'd wake up late, her head pounding, her guts roiling, and she'd call in sick. Today, she seldom misses a day of work. But she still recalls that when she was drinking, the 15 annual sick days she had coming were never near enough to cover the leave she needed for hangovers.

Costs of Alcoholism

Alcohol abuse costs American businesses an estimated $134 billion a year. People with untreated alcohol problems use twice as much sick leave as other employees. They have more on-the-job accidents. They are five times as likely to file a workers' compensation claim.

Addiction research is steadily making progress in identifying the kinds of treatment programs that work for people with a variety of drinking problems. But unhappily, the accumulating scientific evidence on treatment effectiveness rarely translates into appropriate insurance coverage for such addictions. Indeed, addiction coverage typically has caps on both dollar reimbursement and time in treatment. What's more, patients, when they get treatment at all, are often steered into one-size-fits-all programs that don't fit the majority of those in need.

When it comes to treatment for alcohol problems, geography rules. A study by Eric Goplerud of the George Washington University Medical Center found that only seven states require alcohol treatment to be covered at the same level as diabetes, heart disease, and other life-threatening illnesses. And although addicts in those states

Although most alcohol drinkers limit their consumption, many drinkers struggle with addiction.

are more likely to get the treatment they need, even there the mandates are often ignored. Eighteen states have limits on coverage for alcohol problems. In Texas, for example, coverage is required for three "episodes" in a lifetime. Arkansas law sets a lifetime figure of $12,000 for alcohol treatment, and Ohio mandates $550 a year. In much of the country, "insurance either doesn't cover the treatment, or it doesn't cover the right things, or it doesn't cover enough of it," says Goplerud.

Cooper was lucky. Her insurance covered a form of treatment that allowed her to keep working. She never went into a residential treatment program—the type that can keep someone off the job and away from home for 28 days or more. "I was in a 90-day treatment program. I would work until 4 o'clock, then go for treatment from 5 to 9, four days a week. After the first month, it was two days a week," she says. And while Alcoholics Anonymous has been a successful support group for millions, she found meetings with Women For Sobriety to be a better match for her after treatment. "I'm here to tell you that if all they offered me was a 28-day program and AA, I'd

A surgeon implants naltrexone into a patient. The drug treats alcoholism by blocking the pleasurable effects of alcohol.

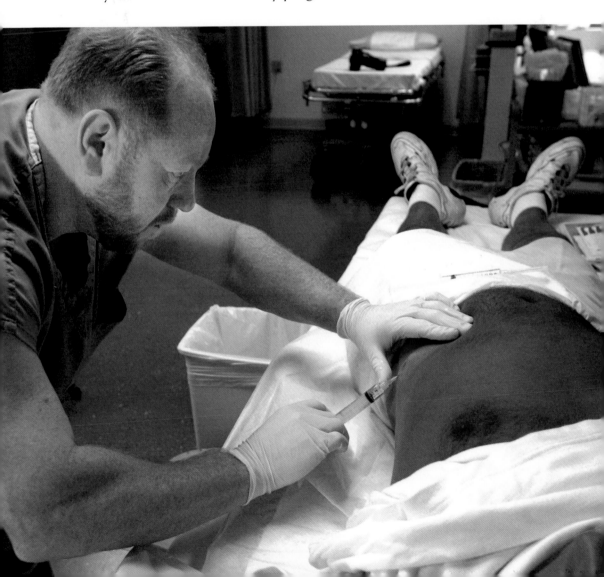

still be drinking," says the 48-year-old Cooper. She now represents drug and alcohol treatment providers at the Pennsylvania Community Providers Association in Harrisburg, Pa.

This alcohol treatment program is geared toward Native Americans and is based on tribal values. It is located in Klamath Falls, Oregon.

The treatment program that worked for Cooper is just one of those described by the American Society of Addiction Medicine [ASAM]. But the problem is that few people have access to such individualized care. "We know a lot about what works," says Michael Flaherty, executive director of the Institute for Research, Education and Training

in Addictions, in Pittsburgh. "The science is 10 years ahead of practice and 15 years ahead of most policy."

Treatment Needs Vary

Everybody's different. Treatment needs vary greatly. Some people need residential treatment for a month or so. Others could benefit from simply using their two weeks of vacation leave for residential treatment, then continuing with outpatient treatment. Still others need less frequent but longer-term outpatient treatment. New medications like the FDA-approved naltrexone and Acamprosate (not yet approved by the agency) can help some drinkers by targeting pathways in the brain and blocking the high that alcoholics seek. Some adults, and almost all adolescents, need social or psychiatric services as well. Women often need child care and generally do better in female-only treatment programs. And almost everyone has family members who need professional guidance in sorting out the tangle of issues that come with loving an addict.

> ## A Range of Alcoholism Problems
>
> It is clear that standard, one-on-one or group addiction therapy in the United States is not sufficiently comprehensive to deal with the range of alcoholism problems facing it.
>
> Stanton Peele, "Harm Reduction in Clinical Practice," *Counselor: The Magazine for Addiction Professionals,* August 1, 2002.

Employers who purchase insurance plans typically don't buy coverage for all the options. And their workplaces reflect the nation's drinking problems. For example, a corporation with 10,000 workers will have an average of 600 employees with alcohol problems. Of those, 30 will receive treatment in a given year, and 22 will be employable a year later. But a company's human resources department could choose differently. It could pay the insurance company to provide outreach services, which would identify twice as many problem drinkers and encourage them to seek treatment. The net result for the company would be 40 employees still on the job a year later. "We know the relationship between amount of services and aftercare and outcomes. We know if we want 40 of 60

Many women feel more secure in female-only treatment programs.

people employable, [insurers] have to fund six months of aftercare," says psychologist Norman Hoffmann of Brown University. Hoffmann helped develop widely used criteria for diagnosis and treatment of alcoholism. Unfortunately, few employers are even aware of the variety of treatment options they should be shopping for when choosing an insurer, says David Mee-Lee, chair of ASAM and editor of the organization's treatment guidelines. . . .

Ironically, the medical consequences associated with heavy drinking, such as cancer, stroke, cirrhosis of the liver, and injuries from falls and traffic accidents, are all typically covered by insurance. Indeed, alcohol abuse adds $23 billion to the nation's annual medical tab. When Cooper was drinking heavily, she underwent a brain scan as physicians tried to figure out why she had chronic headaches. She also had numerous tests to unravel the medical mystery of her gastrointestinal disorders. And she fell on several occasions, sometimes requiring medical treatment. At the peak of her drinking, she was downing several bottles of wine a day. Not coincidentally, she says, "My medical file was eight inches thick."

Analyze the essay:

1. In which paragraph is the essay's main argument stated explicitly? What is the connection between the main argument and the story of Lynn Cooper?

2. What point is the author making with the closing paragraph of the article? Do you think it is an effective conclusion? Why or why not?

Section Two:
Model Essays
and Writing
Exercises

Narrative Writing and the Five-Paragraph Essay

Narrative writing is writing that tells a story or describes an event. Stories are often found in essays meant to persuade. The previous section of this book provided you with examples of essays on alcohol. All were persuasive essays that attempted to convince the reader to support specific arguments about alcohol and alcohol policy. In these essays, the authors used evidence to support their points and also told stories in which alcohol played a part. They were using narrative writing.

In the following section you will read some model essays on alcohol that use narrative writing. You will also do exercises that will help you write your own narrative essays. Some of the model essays and the exercises follow a specific structure—the five-paragraph essay. Before you start, this preface will examine some of the components of narrative writing and the components of five-paragraph essays. It will also examine how narrative writing can be used within the five-paragraph model and longer pieces of writing.

Components of Narrative Writing

All stories contain basic components of character, setting, and plot. These components answer the four basic questions of who, when, where, and what—information that readers need to make sense of the story being told.

Characters answer the question of whom the story is about. In a personal narrative using the first person perspective (I went to a party where people were drinking beer), the characters are the writer and whomever he or she encounters. But writers can also tell the story of other people or characters (John Doe went to a party where people were drinking beer) without being part of the story themselves. The setting answers the questions of when and where the story takes place. The more details given about characters and setting, the more the reader learns about them and the author's views toward them. Mark Warnat's first paragraph in Viewpoint Three provides a good example of vividly describing the setting in which a story takes place.

The plot answers the question of what happens to the characters. It often involves conflict or obstacles that a story's character confronts and must somehow resolve. An example: John Doe has to choose between what his friends want and what his parents want in deciding whether to join in the party's beer drinking. Lilian MacDonald and Murdoch MacDonald's plot in Viewpoint Four revolves around their struggle to cut back on their abusive drinking.

Some people distinguish narrative essays from stories in that essays have a point—a general observation, argument, or insight that the author wants to share with the reader. In other words, narrative essays also answer "why" questions: Why did these particular events happen to the character? Why is this story worth retelling? The story's point is the essay's thesis. A narrative essay can be written in a five-paragraph format often used in testing.

Components of the Five-Paragraph Essay

Five-paragraph essays are a form commonly used in school assignments and tests. The five-paragraph essay has one introductory paragraph, a body of three supporting (or explaining) paragraphs in the middle, and a concluding paragraph at the end. The same general pattern of the five-paragraph essay can be used in essays of longer—or shorter—lengths.

The introduction presents the essay's topic and thesis statement. The topic is the issue or subject discussed in the essay. All the essays in this book are about the same topic—alcohol. The thesis or thesis statement is the argument or point that the essay is trying to make about the topic. The essays in this book all have different thesis statements because they are making differing arguments about the consumption of alcoholic beverages.

The thesis statement should be a clear statement that tells the reader what the essay will be about. The titles of the viewpoints in this book are good examples; they each present a specific argument or assertion about alcohol or alcohol policy. A focused thesis statement helps determine what will be in the essay; the subsequent paragraphs develop and support its point.

In addition to presenting the thesis statement, a well-written introductory paragraph captures the attention of the reader and explains why the topic is important. It may provide the reader with background information on the subject matter. It may also "preview" what points will be covered in the following paragraphs.

The introduction is then followed by three supporting paragraphs. These are the main body of the essay. In most persuasive essays, each paragraph presents and develops a discrete argument (subtopic) that supports the thesis of the entire essay. Each paragraph has its own topic sentence that presents the theme for the paragraph rather than the entire essay. Each subtopic is then supported with its own facts, details, and examples. The writer can use various kinds of supporting material and details to back up the topics of each supporting paragraph. These may include statistics, quotations from people with special knowledge or expertise, historical facts, and anecdotes.

The essay's final or concluding paragraph sums up the essay's ideas and reinforces the thesis statement by restating it in some way. It may recall an idea from the introduction or briefly examine the larger implications of the thesis.

Although the final order of these component paragraphs is important, one does not have to write the five-paragraph essay in the order it appears. Some writing instructors urge students to decide on a thesis and write the introductory paragraph first, then use that paragraph to help structure the rest of the essay. Others suggest that the student decide on a working thesis, decide on the three points used to support it, and write the supporting paragraphs first, before finishing with the introductory and concluding paragraphs. That method could be more flexible; if a student researcher finds that the facts and evidence he or she is finding go beyond, or even against, the working thesis, then the thesis statement could be reworded.

Using Narrative Writing in the Five-Paragraph Essay

Narrative writing can be used in persuasive essays in several different ways. Stories can be used in the introductory paragraph(s) to grab the reader's attention and to introduce the thesis. Stories can comprise all or part of the middle paragraphs that are used to support the thesis. They may even be used in concluding paragraphs as a way to restate and reinforce the essay's general point. Narrative essays may focus on one particular story, or may draw upon multiple stories.

A narrative story can also be used as one of several arguments or supporting points. Susan Brink in Viewpoint Six uses the story of Lynn Cooper, statistical evidence, citations of medical studies, and explanations of what different treatment programs exist. Even in five-paragraph essays, a story can serve as one supporting piece of evidence.

Viewpoint Five, on the other hand, is a good example of how a narrative can take up an entire essay and still create and support the author's thesis. The personal essay begins by introducing the main character and provides a straightforward chronological story. The point of the article is that Antabuse helped her overcome her addiction.

The following model essays provide more examples of how to use narrative writing in essays.

Young People Should Avoid Alcohol

Editor's Notes The following model essay discusses alcohol and its potential effects on young people's lives. It is a five-paragraph persuasive essay written to convince the reader that teens should resist experimenting with alcohol. That thesis is expressed in the first paragraph. The middle three paragraphs support and develop that thesis. Each supporting paragraph has its own topic sentence plus supporting details and information. The essay then concludes with a summary of the main points and a call to action (asking the reader to do something).

What makes the essay an example of narrative writing is its first supporting paragraph. The writer takes the story of Karen (as found in Viewpoint One in the previous section) and condenses it into one paragraph that summarizes the essential actions of the story. Karen's story serves as a representative example of what can happen when teens develop a problem with alcohol. Her experiences provide a concrete and specific example of the general point or thesis of the essay. The linking of Karen's experiences and the general thesis—that drinking alcohol is a potential danger that teens should avoid—continues through the rest of the essay.

As you read this essay, take note of its components and how they are organized (the sidebar notes provide further information on the essay). In addition, consider the following questions:

1. How are the themes of the essay previewed in the introductory paragraph?
2. How are Karen's experiences utilized by the writer in paragraphs three and four?
3. Would the essay be as effective if it contained only general arguments and Karen's story were not included?

Drinking alcohol is against the law for teens, yet that has not stopped many young people from choosing to try it. Unfortunately, many of them have had their lives harmed or ruined by alcohol as a result. Alcohol can cause problems in two areas that are important for any teen—health and family. This is especially true when a teen loses control over his or her drinking.

The story of Karen, a high school student from New York City, provides one example of how alcohol can take control of a person. Karen had tried alcohol on occasion ever since she was four years old. When she was fourteen she began to drink heavily every single day for nine months. Her body became physically dependent on getting that next alcoholic drink. She became more isolated from her parents as she lied to them and defied their curfews and other rules. Finally, her parents confronted her, forced her to come clean about her drinking problem, and sent her to an outpatient treatment program. She also began attending Alcoholics Anonymous (AA) meetings, where she could share her problems with other recovering alcoholics. She suffered some relapses, waking up some mornings lying in her own vomit. But eventually Karen was able to end her drinking. By her senior year she was thinking about what college to go to while continuing to attend AA meetings. She also counsels other young alcoholics.

Karen's story provides one example of how alcohol can affect a person's physical and mental health. Alcohol has several harmful effects on the body, especially when it is abused. Some of the effects are immediate and unpleasant, such as the times Karen woke up lying in her own vomit after a night of binge drinking. But alcohol also carries long-term risks. It can damage the liver, pancreas, and stomach. Heavy drinking can increase the risk for several kinds of cancers, including breast cancer and cancer of the mouth and esophagus. Alcohol also has long-term effects on the brain and body that make people crave the next drink and become dependent on alcohol.

For people with clinical depression—something Karen struggled with—alcohol abuse can interfere with a person's ability to function and overcome that depression. Alcohol can temporarily relieve depression's symptoms, but they come back when alcohol's effects wear off, leaving the person feeling worse.

Karen's experiences also illustrate another way alcohol can affect a person's life—by isolating problem drinkers from families and friends. Many teens like Karen drink in secret even as alcohol becomes a central passion of their lives, thus isolating them from their families. Efforts by family and loved ones to control or monitor a person's drinking can create fights and angry confrontations as alcoholics hide or deny that they have a drinking problem. For Karen, it was only after confronting and treating her alcohol dependency that she was able to recreate a "loving, trusting relationship" with her parents "for the first time in years."

Karen was eventually able to recover from her alcohol addiction, but only after several years of treatment and therapy. The lost years, the pain she caused her family, and whatever harm she did to her body are costs that could have been prevented had she avoided alcohol in the first place. Karen's experiences—and the experiences of many teens like her—should be reason enough to dissuade young people from experimenting with alcohol.

Fourth paragraph examines the topic of how alcohol affects relationships, again using Karen's previously told story as a springboard.

Direct quotations can be a useful tool in writing both persuasive and narrative essays.

Concluding paragraph restates the end of Karen's story while restating the thesis that alcohol can be harmful.

Exercise One

Create an Outline from an Existing Essay

When you write an essay, it often helps to create an outline first. This helps you organize your thoughts and the information you have found in your research. Once you have a good outline, you can fill in the supporting information and, except for polishing your writing, your essay is nearly finished.

To practice, this exercise allows you to deconstruct Essay One. By doing this, you will see how the information is organized. This will help you when you write an outline for your own essay.

Part of the outline has already been started to give you an idea of the assignment.

Outline for Essay One: Young People Should Avoid Alcohol

I. Paragraph 1/essay thesis statement: Many teens have harmed and lost control of their lives by drinking alcohol.
   A. Supporting ideas:
      1. Alcohol harms health.
      2. Alcohol creates family estrangement.
      3. Alcohol is harmful when it takes control of one's life.

II. Paragraph 2: Topic sentence: The story of Karen . . . provides one example of how alcohol can take control. . . .
   A. Events:
      1. Karen drinks at an early age; heavily at age 14.
      2. Consequences of Karen's drinking:
         a) body dependent on alcohol
         b) alienated from parents

        3. Parents confront Karen.
        4. Karen begins treatment.
        5. After relapses, Karen succeeds in recovery.
III. Paragraph 3: Topic sentence:
    A. alcohol's immediate effects
        1. Karen waking up in vomit
    B.
    C.
    D.
IV. Paragraph 4: Topic sentence:
    A.
    B.
    C.
V. Conclusion: Topic sentence:

One Family's Tragedy: A Tale of Drunk Driving

Editor's Notes The second model essay is written in five paragraphs. Its organization is somewhat different than the previous essay, however. Like the first essay, it uses a narrative—the Kelly family's story—to support an argument; in this case, that drunk driving is a menace. However, instead of one supporting paragraph, the story takes up most of the essay. It provides a possible model for organizing a narrative essay.

The first paragraph tells the reader the general point that the story is meant to illustrate. It quickly establishes the setting of the story (time and place). It also briefly foreshadows what will be told in the following paragraphs, without explicitly giving away the ending.

The second paragraph introduces the reader to the main characters in the story—the Kelly family. It provides details, some background, and quotations that enable the reader to get to know the characters better. It also establishes the characters as people worthy of interest and sympathy—the reader is supposed to care about them. Getting the readers emotionally involved in the characters is a hallmark of good storytelling, both fictional and nonfictional.

With the characters and general setting established, the next paragraph begins the action of the story. It describes various events in chronological order. The following paragraph takes us to the central action—the key moment or plot point—of the story. The last paragraph describes the ramifications of what happened after that key action—how the characters were affected. It closes with a general conclusion that the author wants readers to get out of the story.

The notes in the sidebar provide questions that will help you analyze how this essay is organized and how it is written.

Drunk driving is a menace that can strike without warning. In the early morning hours of December 1, 2001, this menace forever changed the lives of the Kelly household in Rhode Island. Their story, as recounted by Madeline Drexler in a *Good Housekeeping* article, illustrates the human costs of society's failure to keep impaired and dangerous drivers off the nation's roads.

Ellen Kelly lived with her daughters Brigid and Elise in a small house in an Irish neighborhood in Newport, Rhode Island. Since her divorce, she had earned a college degree and gotten a job as a fourth-grade teacher. While not rich, her family grew up together rich in love and camaraderie. "We had tough times, which brought us closer together," she later said. She and her daughters called themselves the Kelly girls, swapped clothes, and shopped together. Brigid, the older daughter, who looked like her blond mother, was an honor roll student and a gifted athlete who liked track, cheerleading, and Irish step dancing. When asked to compile a list of friends to call in case of emergency, she came up with forty-eight names.

On November 30, 2001, the family celebrated Elise's seventeenth birthday. Then Brigid left for a Christmas party a half hour's drive away. "Have a good time. Be careful," was Ellen's farewell to her daughter. Brigid was careful, spending the night with friends rather than driving home late at night. The next morning she got up and began the drive to Salve Regina University, where she was a sophomore. There was no forewarning of the tragedy soon to come.

Brigid was driving north on Route 1, a four-lane road, in a Toyota Corolla. Wayne Winslow was traveling in the opposite direction, driving more than one hundred miles an hour in a stolen dark blue van. Winslow was driving with a suspended license, had been drinking the night before, and also had cocaine and heroin in his system. At around 8:40 A.M. Winslow, his driving ability impaired by the chemicals in his system, rammed his vehicle into a minivan. The impact caused the van to spin, cross the

First sentence provides a general thesis. The rest of the essay provides a particular example.

This is one way of acknowledging where you got your story or information.

This paragraph introduces us to the main protagonists and setting of the story. It includes descriptive details of Brigid and her family.

Third paragraph sets the plot in motion—the chronological actions and events that happen to the characters.

Concluding sentence foreshadows what happens next.

This paragraph describes the pivotal or plot point of the story—the accident that killed Brigid.

median, and hit Brigid Kelly's car. The mother and children in the minivan and Winslow himself survived the accident, but Brigid was killed instantly.

This paragraph explains the consequences of the pivotal event of the previous paragraph—consequences that are the topic of the essay.

The accident left Winslow with facial lacerations and ultimately resulted in a guilty plea of several criminal counts of driving under the influence. He was sentenced to seventeen years in prison. The consequences for Ellen and Elise were more severe. They lost not only a daughter and sister, but also a friend. Years later, Ellen continued to wear Brigid's jewelry and to take daily walks on the local beach while talking to her late daughter about what she and Elise have been doing, how she continued to miss her, and that she was proud of her. "And then I cry." It is Ellen's tears—and the tears of people with similar stories—that should be remembered by those charged with making and enforcing laws against the drinking-and-driving menace.

Last sentence echoes the first sentence and returns to the general thesis that drunk driving is a harmful menace.

Exercise Two

Identifying and Organizing Components of the Narrative Essay

As you read in the section preface, all narratives contain certain elements, including characters, setting, and plot. This exercise will help you identify these elements and place them in an organized structure of paragraphs.

For this exercise you may use one of the stories featured in a viewpoint in the previous section. You may also use stories taken from articles or books in the bibliography, or from your own research. You may also, if you choose, use experiences from your own life or those of your friends. Essays drawn from memories or personal experiences are called personal narratives.

Part A: Isolate and write down story elements

Setting:

The setting of a story is the time and place the story happens. Such information helps orient the reader: Does the story take place in the distant or recent past? Does it take place in a typical American community or exotic locale?

Essay Two	story taken from this volume	story from personal experience
Newport, Rhode Island Irish neighborhood November/ December 2001		

Character notes:

Who is the story about? If there is more than one character, how are they related? At what stage of life are they? What are their aspirations and hopes? What makes them distinctive/interesting to the reader?

Essay Two	story taken from this volume	story from personal experience
Ellen Kelly, single mother, teacher, two daughters— Brigid and Elise; Brigid, honor student, athlete; family not rich, but close-knit— swapped clothes, shopped together.		

Pivotal event:

Most stories contain at least one single, discrete event that provides the fulcrum of the narrative. It can be a turning point that changes lives or a specific time when a character confronts a challenge, comes to a flash of understanding, or resolves a conflict.

Essay Two	story taken from this volume	story from personal experience
Brigid is killed in a drunk driving accident.		

Events/actions leading up to the pivotal event:

What are the events that happen to the characters? What are the actions the characters take? These elements are usually told in chronological order in a way that advances the action—that is, each event proceeds naturally and logically from the preceding one.

Essay Two	story taken from this volume	story from personal experience
Family celebrates Elise's birthday. Brigid leaves for Xmas party. She drives next morning to school. She drives toward Wayne Winslow, traveling in opposite direction.		

Events/actions that stem from pivotal event:
What events/actions are the results of the pivotal event in the story? How were the lives of the characters of the stories changed?

Essay Two	story taken from this volume	story from personal experience
Winslow has injuries/prison sentence. Ellen and Elise lose daughter/ sister. Ellen copes with grief by holding conversations.		

Part B: Writing down the elements in paragraph form
One possible (not universal) way of organizing the story elements you have structured is as follows:

Paragraph 1: Tell the reader the setting of the story and introduce the characters. Provide descriptive details of both.

Paragraph 2: Begin the plot—what happens in the story. Tell the events in chronological order, with each event advancing the action.

Paragraph 3: Describe the pivotal event in detail, and its immediate aftermath.

Paragraph 4: Tell the short-term and/or long-term ramifications of the pivotal event.

My Encounter with Sangria

Editor's Notes This essay, unlike the first two, is more than five paragraphs. Sometimes five paragraphs are simply not enough to adequately develop an idea. It also differs in several other ways. The topic is introduced in the beginning, but the thesis or point of the essay is not provided until the end, and even there it is implied rather than explicitly stated. It also differs from the others in being a personal narrative. Rather than based on research or the retelling of someone else's experiences, most of the essay consists of an autobiographical story that recounts memories of an event that happened to the writer involving alcohol and describes the event's significance to that person and what he learned. The essay is written in the subjective or first-person ("I") point of view. Similar essays involving personal narratives can be found in Viewpoints Three, Four, and Five in the previous section.

The sidebars provide additional information and pertinent questions to help you read and take note of the essay's features.

The opening sentence is a takeoff on what people say at AA meetings.

What problem is being introduced in this paragraph? How does the rest of the essay relate back to this question?

My name is Bill, and I am not an alcoholic.

I am not alone in my condition, of course. But 14 million Americans do have a problem with alcoholism or heavy drinking, according to the National Institute on Alcohol Abuse and Alcoholism. Sometimes I wonder how I have managed to avoid being one of those people. Looking back on my life, I can think of several reasons.

Perhaps my parents deserve credit. Some studies show that alcoholism can be an inherited condition, and my parents are not alcoholics. In addition to the genes they have given me, my parents also taught me and my siblings that alcohol was not for children. They drank some, but not much, and thus showed me by example that people can lead happy productive lives without having to have a drink every day.

Perhaps my experiences at school are a reason. I paid attention in health classes when they taught that alcohol was a dangerous drug. I took to heart the movies they showed about teenagers who drank alcohol and whose lives became a mess. I was a good student. I was also shy and did not socialize much. Other parents may have worried about their high school kids going to unsupervised parties where alcohol may have been served. My mom used to worry about me because I *wasn't* going to any parties, supervised or unsupervised. At least, that's what she pestered me about.

So there is probably a combination of different reasons why I have managed to avoid having a drinking problem. But if someone were to ask me to say in one word why I am not an alcoholic, the answer would be: sangria.

I had never heard of sangria until I was out of college and away from my family. I lived in a house I shared with three other guys to split the rent. We got along okay, even though they were the type of people who went to the cool parties in high school and I was not. Part of me still felt a bit left out. So I was happy when they invited me to try out a downtown restaurant one Friday night. We went to a place with a Spanish theme. It had colorful décor, served appetizers called tapas, and a beverage called sangria. We sat and ate and talked—and drank.

Sangria, I later found out, is a mixture of wine, brandy, fruit, spices, and soda water. I remember the waitresses bringing it out in big painted ceramic pitchers filled with a bright red liquid with the fruit floating on top. It tasted like sweet yet tart fruit juice. I drank my glass, poured some more out of the carafe, and drank some more. I was thirsty, the food was spicy, and someone else was driving that night. Perhaps a small part of me was also thinking that this was a chance to really get that alcohol "buzz"

> What does the reader learn about the narrator in these two paragraphs? What function do they have in the essay?

> These sentences help set the stage for the following story.

> What elements of character and setting are provided by the writer in this paragraph?

> What is the pivotal event or "moment of truth" in this narrative?

> A person's internal thoughts can help reveal character and advance the plot—what the character decides to do and why.

I read and heard about. Yes, I thought to myself, maybe I could really experience that warm flushed glow of an alcohol high and catch up on whatever it was I missed by not going to those parties in high school.

In those high school health classes they talked about how alcohol affects different parts of the brain. I remember learning that alcohol affects the part of the brain that controls judgment and reasoning, and the parts of the brain that control speech. What I do not remember learning is how alcohol affects the part of the brain that controls your sense of equilibrium. But that night, just as I was thinking that this sangria stuff was really good, everything just started spinning. If I shut my eyes, it felt like I was sitting on a barstool that was turning faster and faster. I opened my eyes and tried to tell myself that this was not happening and that my chair was not spinning, but to no avail. I stopped talking. I stopped drinking and eating. I stared straight ahead. I concentrated on a picture of a flower on the wall and stared at it. I prayed. Make the spinning stop. Make the spinning stop.

After a while the spinning slowed down. I would try to talk and eat again, but I would then lose my concentration and things would start spinning faster again. I tried not to say anything or complain to my housemates. Eventually we all went home and I lay down in bed. That was a mistake because the whole bed started spinning over and around me. I spent a miserable night sitting up and staring across the room, trying to make the spinning stop. I had to make several emergency trips to the toilet, stumbling and lurching dizzily across the hallway. I did not always make it in time.

My housemates and I joked about that evening for several days afterward. But my encounter with sangria that night did have a lasting effect on me. It confirmed for me what I had already suspected: Whatever it was that alcohol provided to other people it could not provide to me—at least, not without getting me dizzy first.

How are the consequences described in this paragraph a result of decisions made earlier in the story?

Sometimes, descriptive details are best left implied rather than expressed.

What lesson does the author derive from his experience? How does it answer the question at the beginning of the essay?

Maybe it is those parental genes after all. Many alcoholics, I suspect, got that way because they got dizzy with happiness when they tried alcohol, so they drink again and again, every day, to recapture those feelings. For me, I just get dizzy.

But I Can't Write That

One aspect about personal narrative writing is that you are revealing to the reader something about yourself. Many people enjoy this part of writing. Others are not so sure about sharing their personal stories—especially if they reveal something embarrassing or something that could get them in trouble. What are your options?

- Talk with your teacher about your concerns. Will this narrative be shared in class? Can the teacher pledge confidentiality?
- Change the story from being about "I" to a story about "a friend" or "a person I know." This will involve writing in the third person rather than the first person.
- Change a few identifying details and names to disguise characters and settings.
- Pick a different topic or thesis that you do not mind sharing.

Exercise Three

Writing a Five-Paragraph Essay with Narrative Elements

The final exercise is to write your own five-paragraph (or longer) essay. Now it is time to write your own essay on alcohol. Here are six steps to help you organize your work:

1. Appendix C lists topics and writing prompts relating to alcohol. Choose one topic from the list, or make up your own. Think about what it is that you want to persuade your readers to do or think. State your idea as a thesis sentence.

Remember that the thesis statement has two parts: the topic (whatever aspect of alcohol you chose in step one) and the point of the essay. Through the thesis, you are announcing your topic to the reader and stating what you believe is significant about that topic. The thesis helps organize and determine the content of the rest of the essay.

2. Now you need to find stories and other information to help you make your case. You can find information in the viewpoints and essays in this book; at a library; on the Internet; and in newspapers, magazines, encyclopedias, books, and speeches. You can also use the resources listed in the appendices "Bibliography" and "Organizations to Contact." (See Appendix B, "Finding and Using Sources of Information," for more information on this topic.)

In your research for this assignment, look especially for personal stories and narratives. Try to paraphrase the stories in 1- or 2-paragraph form, providing essential information on setting, character, and plot. Include the general point of the story and see whether it supports the thesis statement you created in step 1.

3. After you have read and thought about the information you have found, decide what three main ideas and/or anecdotes will best support your thesis.

(Be aware that at this point you might have to adjust your thesis sentence. In your research you might have found information that makes you want to take a different approach. That is OK. You do not want to stick with a thesis statement that you cannot support properly.)

Write your three main supporting ideas/stories.

4. Decide how you can most effectively use the information you found. Could the thesis be supported by one or more brief anecdotes, each of which could take up one paragraph? Would such anecdotes work with other paragraphs of persuasive evidence, such as facts and statistics? Or would it be better to develop one story at length, with three or more paragraphs, as the main and only support of the thesis?

5. Now, write a simple outline for your essay. (Adjust the length of this outline to fit your essay.) You could use either one of the following structural templates.

I. Thesis statement
   A. Supporting idea 1   or   A. Characters/setting of story
   B. Supporting idea 2   or   B. Pivotal event of story
   C. Suppporting idea 3   or   C. Ramification of pivotal event

II. Paragraph 2: Topic sentence
   A. First evidence   or   A. Description of characters
   B. Second evidence   or   B. Description of setting
   C. Third evidence
   D. Fourth evidence

III. Paragraph 3: Topic sentence
   A. First evidence   or   A. Plot event 1, leading to
   B. Second evidence   or   B. Plot event 2, leading to
   C. Third evidence   or   C. Plot event 3, leading to
   D. Fourth evidence   or   D. Pivotal event

IV. Paragraph 4: Topic sentence
   A. First evidence   or   A. Ramification 1 of pivotal event
   B. Second evidence or   B. Ramification 2 of pivotal event
   C. Third evidence   or   C. Summary of where characters end up

V. Conclusion: Topic sentence; or Conclusion, general point of story

6. Now flesh out your essay with the information you have found and the stories you have decided to use. Don't forget to think about a way to catch your reader's attention in the first paragraph, use transitions to make your essay move smoothly from one idea to the next, and make your final paragraph a strong last pitch for your idea.

Section Three: Supporting Research Material

Facts About Alcohol

Editor's Note: These facts can be used in reports or papers to reinforce or add credibility when making important points or claims.

What Is Alcohol?

- There are many types of alcohol. Ethyl alcohol, or ethanol, is the one found in alcoholic beverages. It is produced by fermentation. Yeast is added to sugars to produce alcohol and carbon dioxide.
- Ethanol is also used for nondrinking purposes, such as gasoline additive or chemical solvent. Manufacturers of commercial ethanol often add poisonous chemicals to make it undrinkable.
- Alcohol is a drug that is categorized as a depressant. As such, it decreases the activity of the central nervous system and makes the user feel calm, entranced, and drowsy. In large doses it can cause drunkenness, a state of impaired physical and mental faculties.
- There are two general types of alcoholic beverages. Fermented drinks, such as beer and wine, contain 5 to 20 percent alcohol. Distilled drinks, such as brandy, rum, gin, and vodka contain 12 to 55 percent alcohol.

Alcohol Consumption in the United States

- In 2001 the average per capita annual consumption of alcoholic beverages in the United States was 25 gallons per person. That figure peaked in 1981 at 28.8 gallons. (Source: Economic Research Department of the U.S. Department of Agriculture.)
- 81.7 percent of Americans twelve and over (184.4 million people) have tried alcoholic beverages at least once.
- 85 percent of Americans between the ages of eighteen and twenty-five have tried alcohol at some point in their lives.

- 42.9 percent of Americans aged twelve to seventeen have tried alcohol at some time in their lives.
- 63.7 percent of Americans (143.6 million people) drank alcohol sometime in the past year.
- 48.3 percent of Americans (109 million) used alcohol in the past month.
  (Source: National Household Survey on Drug Abuse, 2001, Substance Abuse and Mental Health Services Administration.)

Underage Drinking

- Alcohol is the number-one drug of choice among children and adolescents, ranking above tobacco and illegal drugs.
- In 2002 about 2 million youths aged twelve through twenty drank five or more drinks on an occasion five or more times a month, and more than 7 million reported this level of consumption at least once in the survey month.
- Alcohol use by persons under age twenty-one poses both short-term and long-term risks:
  - In 2002, 1.5 million youths aged twelve through seventeen were in need of alcohol treatment. Of these, only 120,000 received treatment.
  - Alcohol is the leading cause of death for persons under age twenty-one.
  - Each year about nineteen hundred persons under the age of twenty-one die in motor vehicle crashes that involve underage drinking.
  - Alcohol is also involved in about sixteen hundred homicides and three hundred suicides among persons under age twenty-one.
  - About sixteen hundred persons under age twenty-one die from alcohol-related unintentional injuries (not related to motor vehicle crashes).
  - Forty percent of those who start drinking before the age of fifteen become dependent on alcohol at some point in their lives.

- Research indicates that the human brain continues to develop into a person's early twenties and that exposure of the developing brain to alcohol may have long-lasting effects on intellectual capabilities and may increase the likelihood of alcohol addiction.
  (Source: National Institute on Alcohol Abuse and Alcoholism.)

Drunk Driving

- Alcohol-related motor vehicle crashes kill someone every thirty-one minutes and nonfatally injure someone every two minutes.
- During 2003, 17,013 people in the United States died in alcohol-related motor vehicle crashes, representing 40 percent of all traffic-related deaths.
- Of the 2,136 traffic fatalities among children aged zero to fourteen years in 2003, 21 percent involved alcohol.
- Among drivers involved in fatal crashes, those with BAC levels of 0.08 percent or higher were nine times more likely to have a prior conviction for driving while impaired (DWI) than were drivers who had not consumed alcohol.
  (Source: National Highway Traffic and Safety Administration.)

Facts About Alcohol Abuse and Alcoholism

- Alcoholism is a disease with the following characteristics:
  - It is a chronic disease, meaning it lasts a person's lifetime.
  - It follows a predictable course.
  - It has the following four symptoms:
    1. craving: A strong need, or urge, to drink.
    2. loss of control: Not being able to stop drinking once drinking has begun.
    3. physical dependence: Withdrawal symptoms, such as nausea, sweating, shakiness, and anxiety after stopping drinking.

4. tolerance: The need to drink greater amounts of alcohol to get "high."

- Alcoholism runs in families.
- Genes play a role in transmitting the disease, but other factors—such as lifestyle and stress—contribute to a person's risk of becoming alcoholic.
- Not every child of an alcoholic becomes an alcoholic; conversely, people with no family history of alcoholism can become alcoholics.
- Alcoholism cannot be cured, but it can be effectively treated with counseling and medication.
- A person can abuse alcohol without becoming an alcoholic: They may drink too much and experience problems with alcohol without actually becoming physically dependent on alcohol.
- Some of the problems linked to alcohol abuse include not being able to meet work, school, or family responsibilities; drunk-driving arrests and car crashes; and drinking-related medical conditions.
- Under some circumstances, even social or moderate drinking is dangerous; for example, when driving, during pregnancy, or when taking certain medications.
- Nearly 14 million people in the United States—one in every thirteen adults—abuse alcohol or are alcoholic.
- In general, more men than women are alcohol dependent or have alcohol problems. Alcohol problems are highest among young adults aged eighteen to twenty-nine and lowest among adults aged sixty-five and older.
- People who start drinking at an early age—for example, at age fourteen or younger—greatly increase the chance that they will develop alcohol problems at some point in their lives.
(Source: The National Institute on Alcohol Abuse and Alcoholism.)

Finding and Using Sources of Information

It is possible to write personal narratives using only one's own memories. But when you write a narrative involving other people, or as part of a persuasive essay, it is usually necessary to find information to support your point of view. You can use sources such as books, magazine articles, newspaper articles, and online articles.

Using Books and Articles

You can find books and articles in a library by using the library's cataloging system. If you are not sure how to use these resources, ask a librarian to help you. You can also use a computer to find many magazine articles and other articles written specifically for the Internet.

You are likely to find a lot more information than you can possibly use in your essay, so your first task is to narrow it down to what is likely to be most usable. Look at book and article titles. Look at book chapter titles, and take a look at the book index to see if the book contains information on the specific topic you want to write about. (For example, if you want to write about underage drinking and you find a book about alcohol abuse, check the chapter titles and index to be sure it contains information about underage drinking before you bother to check out the book.)

For a five-paragraph essay, you do not need a great deal of supporting information, so quickly try to narrow down your materials to a few good books and magazine or Internet articles. You do not need dozens. You might even find that one or two good books or articles contain all the information you need.

You probably do not have time to read an entire book, so find the chapters or sections that relate to your topic, and skim these. When you find useful information, copy it onto a notecard or notebook. You should look for supporting facts, statistics, quotations, and examples.

Evaluate the Source

When you select your supporting information, it is important that you evaluate its source. This is especially important with information you find on the Internet. Because nearly anyone can put information on the Internet, there is as much bad information as good information. Before using Internet information—or any information—try to determine if the source is reliable. Is the author or Internet site sponsored by a legitimate organization? Is it from a government source? Does the author have any special knowledge or training relating to the topic you are looking up? Does the article give any indication of where its information comes from?

Using Your Supporting Information

When you use supporting information from a book, article, interview, or other source, there are three important things to remember:

1. Make it clear whether you are using a direct quotation or a paraphrase. If you copy information directly from your source, you are quoting it. You must put quotation marks around the information and tell where the information comes from. If you put the information in your own words, you are paraphrasing it.

Here is an example of using a quotation:

Michael J. Lemanski argues that Alcoholics Anonymous and other self-help groups provide to alcoholics "the antithesis of therapy. There is no cure; the solution provided by such programs entails an endless attendance at meetings." [1]

1. Michael J. Lemanski, "The Tenacity of Error in Treatment of Addiction," *Humanist*, May/June 1997.

Here is an example of a brief paraphrase of the same passage:

Michael J. Lemanski contends that Alcoholics Anonymous and other self-help organizations do not provide therapy or cure alcoholism, but simply replace addiction to alcohol with a new addiction to attending recovery groups.

2. Use the information fairly. Be careful to use supporting information in the way the author intended it. There is a joke that movie ads containing critics' comments like "First-Class!" "Best ever!" and other glowing phrases take them from longer reviews that say something like "This movie is first-class trash," or "This movie is this director's best ever—and that isn't saying much!" This is called taking information out of context (using it in a way the original writer did not intend). This is using supporting evidence unfairly.

3. Give credit where credit is due. You must give credit when you use someone else's information, but not every piece of supporting information needs a credit.
   • If the supporting information is general knowledge—that is, it can be found in many sources—you do not have to cite (give credit to) your source.
   • If you directly quote a source, you must give credit.
   • If you paraphrase information from a specific source, you must give credit.
   If you do not give credit where you should, you are plagiarizing—or stealing—someone else's work.
   There are a number of ways to give credit. Your teacher will probably want you to do it one of three ways:
   • Informal: Tell where you got the information in the same place you use it.
   • Informal list: At the end of the article, place an unnumbered list of the sources you used. This tells the reader where, in general, you got your informa-

tion, but it doesn't tell specifically where you got any single fact.

- Formal: Use a footnote, like the first example in number 1 above. (A footnote is generally placed at the end of an article or essay, although it may be located in different places depending on your teacher's requirements.)

Generally, the very least information needed is the original author's name and the name of the article or other publication. Be sure you know exactly what information your teacher requires before you start looking for your supporting information so that you know what information to include with your notes.

Sample Essay Topics and Writing Prompts

General
Alcohol Abuse Is a Serious Problem
The Alcohol Industry Should Be Taxed to Pay for Alcohol-Related Social Problems
The Alcohol Industry Is Being Unfairly Targeted
Youth Drinking Is a Serious Problem
Alcohol Advertising Should Be Banned
Alcohol Advertising Should Not Be Banned

Alcohol and Driving
Drunk Driving Is Dangerous
Alcohol and Driving Should Never Mix
Drunk Driving Laws Have Gone Too Far

Alcohol and Teens
Drinking Age Laws Are Fair
Drinking Age Laws Are Unfair
Teens Can Drink Responsibly
Teens Cannot Drink Responsibly
Peer Pressure Affects Alcohol Use
Parental Messages Affect Teen Alcohol Use
Advertising Affects Teen Alcohol Use

Alcoholism Treatment and Recovery
Alcoholism Is a Serious Disease
Alcoholism Is Not a Disease
Alcoholics Anonymous Meetings Can Help Alcoholics
Alcoholics Anonymous Does Not Help Alcoholics
Medication Can Help Alcoholics
Intervention Can Help Alcoholics
Alcoholics Must Take Responsibility for Their Drinking

Writing Prompts

Use another person's story, derived from research, to argue for or against the proposition that underage drinking is always harmful.

Describe what happened during an incident when you or a person you know faced the choice of whether to consume alcohol or not, and what influenced that decision. Using research, interviews, or personal experience, tell the story of a person who developed a drinking problem and was able to overcome it (or not).

Organizations to Contact

Al-Anon Family Group Headquarters
1600 Corporate Landing Pkwy., Virginia Beach, VA 23454
(757) 563-1600 • fax: (757) 563-1655
Web site: www.al-anon.al-ateen.org

Al-Anon is a fellowship of men, women, and children
whose lives have been affected by an alcoholic family
member or friend.

Alcoholics Anonymous (AA)
General Service Office, PO Box 459, Grand Central Station,
New York, NY 10163 • (212) 870-3400
fax: (212) 870-3003 • Web site: www.aa.org

Alcoholics Anonymous is an international fellowship of
people who are recovering from alcoholism.

American Beverage Institute (ABI)
1775 Pennsylvania Ave. NW, Suite 1200, Washington, DC
20006 • (202) 463-7110 • Web site: www.abionline.org

The American Beverage Institute is a restaurant industry
trade organization that works to protect the consumption
of alcoholic beverages in the restaurant setting.

Center on Alcohol Marketing and Youth
2233 Wisconsin Ave. NW, Suite 525, Washington, DC
20007 • (202) 687-1019 • e-mail: info@camy.org
Web site: www.camy.org

The Center on Alcohol Marketing and Youth at Georgetown
University is a nonprofit organization that monitors the
marketing practices of the alcohol industry to focus attention and action on industry practices that it believes jeop-
ardize the health and safety of America's youth.

Hazelden Foundation
PO Box 176, 15251 Pleasant Valley Rd., Center City, MN
55012-9640 • toll-free: (800) 329-9000

e-mail: info@hazelden.org • Web site: www.hazelden.org

The Hazelden Foundation is a nonprofit organization that runs a network of drug and alcohol rehabilitation centers and publishes pamphlets and books on alcoholism.

Mothers Against Drunk Driving (MADD)

511 E. John Carpenter Frwy., Suite 700, Irving, TX 75062
toll-free: 800-GET-MADD (438-6233)
fax: (972) 869-2206/07 • e-mail: Information: info@madd.org.
e-mail: Victim's Assistance: victims@madd.org
Web site: www.madd.org

MADD provides materials for use in medical facilities and health and driver education programs.

National Institute on Alcoholism and Alcohol Abuse

5635 Fishers Ln., MSC 9304, Bethesda, MD 20892-9304
Web site: www.niaaa.nih.gov

The National Institute on Alcoholism and Alcohol Abuse, part of the National Institutes of Health, publishes pamphlets, brochures, and posters dealing with alcohol abuse and alcoholism.

Rational Recovery Systems (RRS)

PO Box 800, Lotus, CA 95651
(530) 621-2667 • e-mail: rrsn@rational.org
Web site: www.rational.org/recovery

RRS is a national self-help organization that offers a cognitive rather than spiritual approach to recovery from alcoholism.

Responsibility in DUI Laws (RIDL)

PO Box 87053, Canton, MI 48188
e-mail: info@ridl.us • Web site: www.ridl.us

RIDL is an organization that works to raise public awareness of current trends in DUI laws that the organization believes have little effect toward curbing drunk driving, but instead result in criminalizing and punishing responsible drinkers.

Bibliography

Books

Magdalena Alagna, *Everything You Need to Know About the Dangers of Binge Drinking*. New York: Rosen, 2001.

Alcoholics Anonymous, *Alcoholics Anonymous*. 4th ed. New York: Alcoholics Anonymous World Service, 2000.

Griffith Edwards, *Alcohol: The World's Favorite Drug*. New York: Thomas Dunne, 2002.

Anne M. Fletcher, *Sober for Good: New Solutions for Drinking Problems—Advice from Those Who Have Succeeded*. Boston: Houghton Mifflin, 2002.

Katherine Ketcham et al., *Beyond the Influence: Understanding and Defeating Alcoholism*. New York: Bantam, 2000.

Cynthia Kuhn et al., *Buzzed: The Straight Facts About the Most Used and Abused Drugs from Alcohol to Ecstasy*. New York: W.W. Norton, 2003.

Jodee Kulp, *The Best I Can Be: Living with Fetal Alcohol Syndrome*. St. Paul, MN: Better Endings, New Beginnings, 2000.

Shelley Marshall, *Young, Sober, and Free: Experience, Strength, and Hope for Young Adults*. Center City, MN: Hazelden, 2003.

Marjana Martinic and Barbara Leigh, *Reasonable Risk: Alcohol in Perspective*. New York: Brunner-Routledge, 2004.

Heather Ogilvie, *Alternatives to Abstinence: A New Look at Alcoholism and Choices in Treatment*. Long Island City, NY: Hatherleigh, 2001.

Edmund B. O'Reilly, *Sobering Tales: Narratives of Alcoholism and Recovery*. Amherst: University of Massachusetts Press, 1997.

Bert Pluymen, *The Thinking Person's Guide to Sobriety*. New York: Griffin, 2000.

Joyce Brennfleck Shannon, ed., *Alcohol Information for Teens*. Detroit: Omnigraphics, 2005.

Barbara Sheen, *Teen Alcoholism*. San Diego: Lucent, 2004.

Koren Zailckas, *Smashed: Story of a Drunken Girlhood*. New York: Viking, 2005.

Periodicals

Janet Arenofsky, "I'll Never Drink and Drive Again," *Current Health 2*, December 1999.

Susan Brink, "Your Brain on Alcohol," *U.S. News & World Report*, May 7, 2001.

Dana Dickey, "The Agony of Growing Up the Daughter of an Alcoholic," *Glamour*, February 2001.

Barbara Ehrenreich, "Libation as Liberation? Going Toe to Toe with Men Is a Feminist Act; Going Drink for Drink with Them Isn't," *Time*, April 1, 2002.

Monique Fields, "A Sobering Place," *Essence*, December 2000.

Melanie Franklin, "My Daughter Was a Drunk Driver," *Good Housekeeping*, August 1998.

Leah Ginsberg, "My Mom Was an Alcoholic," *CosmoGirl!*, April 2002.

Jodie Morse, "Women on a Binge: Many Teen Girls Are Drinking as Much as Boys," *Time*, April 1, 2002.

Stanton Peele, "Drunk with Power: The Case Against Court-Imposed 12-Step Treatments," *Reason*, May 2001.

Dennis Prager, "Jenna Bush Is Old Enough to Drink," *Wall Street Journal*, June 8, 2001.

Patrick Rogers, "Too Much, Too Soon: John Brodhead Started Drinking at Age 11. He's Not Alone," *People Weekly*, August 12, 2002.

San Francisco Chronicle, "Alcohol's Allure," April 6, 2003.

Sora Song, "The High Cost of Teen Drinking," *Time,* September 22, 2003.

Karen Springen and Barbara Kantrowitz, "Alcohol's Deadly Triple Threat: Women Get Addicted Faster, Seek Help Less Often and Are More Likely to Die from the Bottle," *Newsweek,* May 10, 2004.

Gary Stix, "Should Physicians Tell Some Nondrinkers to Start?" *Scientific American,* July 17, 2001.

Michael J. Taleff, "What's the Latest Research on AA?" *Counselor,* December 2003.

Web Sites

Alcohol: Problems and Solutions (www2.potsdam.edu/ alcohol-info). This site features the writings of David J. Hanson, a professor emeritus of sociology at the State University of New York at Potsdam who has studied alcohol and drinking for more than thirty years.

Indiana University, Bloomington, Alcohol Research and Health Information (www.indiana.edu/ ~ engs/index. shtml). This site provides the text of numerous studies on binge drinking, the minimum drinking age, and the health effects of alcohol.

Lowe Family Foundation (www.lowefamily.org). The Lowe Family Foundation is a charitable organization dedicated to providing assistance to people coping with alcohol abuse in their family. The Web site includes interviews with experts on alcohol abuse and a comprehensive listing of alcohol and drug abuse counseling organizations nationwide.

Index

naltrexone, 51
National Institute on Alcohol Abuse and Alcoholism (NIAAA), 13, 18, 70

Prohibition, 14

Saturday Evening Post (magazine), 37

treatment programs, 47–48, 50–51

Vanderkam, Laura, 22

Warnat, Mark, 28
Wechsler, Henry, 23
Winslow, Wayne, 65–66

youth drinking, 12–13, 18–19, 26–27

Picture Credits

About the Editor

William Dudley received his BA degree from Beloit College in Wisconsin, where he majored in English composition and wrote for the school newspaper and literary journal. He has since written and published op-ed pieces, travel articles, and other pieces of writing. He has edited dozens of books on history and social issues for Greenhaven Press at Thomson/Gale.